Vermont
The Green Mountain State

Robin Koontz

PowerKiDS
press™

New York

Published in 2011 by The Rosen Publishing Group, Inc.
29 East 21st Street, New York, NY 10010

First Edition

Editor: Amelie von Zumbusch
Book Design: Greg Tucker
Layout Design: Ashley Burrell
Photo Researcher: Jessica Gerweck

Photo Credits: Cover Zeb Andrews/Getty Images; p. 5 © www.iStockphoto.com/Marcio Silva; p. 7 © North Wind Picture Archives; p. 9 John Phillips/Time Life Pictures/Getty Images; pp. 11, 13, 17, 22 (tree, horse, flower) Shutterstock.com; p. 15 © Kindra Clineff/age fotostock; p. 19 Purestock/Getty Images; p. 22 (John Deere) Wikipedia Commons; p. 22 (Calvin Coolidge) Imagno/Hulton Archive/Getty Images; p. 22 (Hannah Teter) Doug Pensinger/Getty Images.

Library of Congress Cataloging-in-Publication Data

Koontz, Robin Michal.
  Vermont : the Green Mountain State / Robin Koontz. — 1st ed.
      p. cm. — (Our amazing states)
  Includes index.
  ISBN 978-1-4488-0649-2 (library binding) — ISBN 978-1-4488-0730-7 (pbk.) —
ISBN 978-1-4488-0731-4 (6-pack)
  1. Vermont—Juvenile literature. I. Title.
  F49.3.K66 2011
  974.3—dc22
                                        2009050113

Manufactured in the United States of America

CPSIA Compliance Information: Batch #WS10PK: For Further Information contact Rosen Publishing, New York, New York at 1-800-237-9932

Contents

More Trees than People

Which state is known around the world for its **maple syrup**? Vermont! People come to Vermont in spring to watch how this tasty treat is made. In summer, more people come to Vermont. They like to boat, swim, and fish in the state's lakes and rivers. In fall, people come back to Vermont. They want to see the bright colors of the leaves. Vermont's mountains draw thousands of skiers in winter. Its snow-covered trees and mountains make Vermont a wild wonderland!

Vermont is in the group of six states called New England. It is in the northeastern part of the United States. There are only about 600,000 people living in Vermont. That makes Vermont one of the least **populated** states.

4

Vermont's snow-covered mountains are beautiful in winter. They are also great places to go skiing or snowboarding.

The Earliest People

Algonquian Native Americans lived in the Vermont **area**. Most were Abenaki Indians. Some Abenakis lived along a river they named the Winooski River. Others lived along the Connecticut River.

In 1609, French **explorer** Samuel de Champlain came to Vermont. He claimed the land for France. He found a huge lake. He named it Lake Champlain. Champlain also saw the Green Mountains. These mountains likely gave Vermont its name. *Vert* means "green" in French. *Mont* means "mountain." English settlers followed the French. The English claimed land near the Connecticut River. In 1724, they built a fort there. Across North America, English settlers fought with the French and Native Americans over who owned the land. By 1763, the English had won.

These Indians are building homes called wigwams. Many Abenakis built and lived in wigwams. Wigwams have a wood frame covered with tree bark.

Famous Fighters

Soon, English settlers started fighting over Vermont. The English **colonies** of New York and New Hampshire claimed the land there. A small army called the Green Mountain Boys formed in Bennington, Vermont. They fought to be free from New York. Later, the Green Mountain Boys fought in the American Revolution. This was a war that American colonists fought to become free from England. The Green Mountain Boys fought in many key battles, such as the Battle of Bennington.

The Americans won the war in 1781. They formed the United States. However, Vermont became an independent **republic**. In 1791, Vermont became part of the United States. It was the first state to join the 13 **original** states.

On May 10, 1775, the Green Mountain Boys captured New York's Fort Ticonderoga from the British army. It was one of the first battles of the American Revolution.

Mountains and Lakes

Forests cover most of Vermont. The tree-covered Green Mountains are in the center of the state. Vermont's nickname is the Green Mountain State. The mountains have granite, marble, and slate in them. These rocks can be used to make things such as buildings and roofs.

Vermont has lots of rivers. It has about 430 lakes and ponds. Lake Champlain forms part of the state's western border. It is the largest lake in New England.

Vermont's four seasons all have different weather. Its very cold winters lead to wet springs. The spring rains make the ground muddy. Spring in Vermont is often called mud season. The summer heat does not last long. It is cool and sunny in fall.

Vermont's Green Mountains are part of the Appalachian mountains. This long mountain system crosses many states in the eastern United States.

What Lives in Vermont?

Vermont's forests, fields, rivers, and lakes are good places for animals to live. Different animals make their homes in different places. Wild turkeys live in the forests. Woodchucks like fields where they can eat plants. They dig cozy dens there, too. Beavers live near trees and water. They use their big teeth to chop down trees. Beavers build dams with the trees.

There are more than 50 kinds of trees in Vermont. Lots are evergreen trees. These trees keep their thin, green leaves through the winter. There are also many trees that lose their leaves in winter. The most common of these is the sugar maple. People collect sap from sugar maples in spring. They use the sap to make maple syrup.

This Vermont family is gathering sap from a maple tree. They will boil down the sap to make maple syrup. The making of maple syrup is known as sugaring.

A Tasty State

Vermont gets **millions** of visitors each year. They like all the fun things that happen there. Vermont has lots of places where visitors can eat and sleep. Many Vermonters make money that way. People in Vermont also make parts for computers. Factories there make wood **products**, too.

Vermont has lots of farmers who use natural farming methods. They sell naturally grown fruit and vegetables. Many Vermont farmers have **dairy** cows. People in Vermont make cheese from some of their milk. Vermont cheese is sold around the world.

Vermont's best-known dairy product may be ice cream. The first Ben & Jerry's ice-cream shop was in Burlington, Vermont. Today, thousands of people visit the company's factory in Waterbury, Vermont.

Vermont's cheese makers make more than 150 kinds of cheese. The state is best known for the cheddar made there.

Burlington and Montpelier

Montpelier is the capital of Vermont. It is the smallest state capital in the United States. Most of the people in Montpelier work for the government. This pretty city is in the Winooski River valley. It is home to the New England Culinary Institute. People go there to become great **chefs**!

The biggest city in Vermont is Burlington. More than two-thirds of the people in Vermont live in the country. However, most Vermonters who live in a city live in Burlington. Burlington is on the eastern shore of Lake Champlain. Mountains and forests surround the city. The lake, trees, and mountains give the city a beautiful setting. Burlington's Church Street Marketplace is a well-loved stop for shoppers.

The Vermont Statehouse, seen here, was finished in 1859. However, parts of the building come from an earlier statehouse that burned down in 1857.

A Lake with a Mystery

Lake Champlain is big and deep. Vermont is on the lake's eastern side. New York is to the west. The lake's northern tip is in Quebec, Canada. In the past, people fought over who would control the lake. Today, visitors can see forts that were built to guard the lake. Visitors also swim, fish, and sail in the lake. There are remains of old ships on the lake's bottom. **Scuba divers** visit them. Many of these ships are part of the Vermont Underwater Historic Preserve.

Some people say that a **creature** lives in Lake Champlain. The creature is said to look like a giant snake. The Abenakis called it Tatoskok. Others named it Champ. To this day, people report sightings of the creature.

Sailboats, motorboats, kayaks, and canoes are a common sight on Lake Champlain in summer. In winter, though, the lake sometimes freezes. Then, people cannot use boats.

Exploring Vermont

Vermont has 52 state parks. There are places to camp all over the state, even on islands! Campers can hike, bicycle, or climb mountains. Bird-watchers look at the state's many birds. Hikers follow the Long Trail in Vermont. This trail winds from Massachusetts through Vermont to Canada. Vermont is a fun place to take a country drive, too. Many drivers come to see the colorful fall leaves. In winter, people ski and snowboard in the mountains.

Vermonters do not mind having so many visitors. **Tourism** brings a lot of money to the state. Vermonters work to **protect** their state's natural places. That way, both Vermonters and visitors can enjoy the state's natural beauty for years to come.

Glossary

area (ER-ee-uh) A certain space or place.

chefs (SHEFS) Skilled head cooks.

colonies (KAH-luh-neez) Places where people move that are still ruled by the leaders of the country from which they came.

creature (KREE-chur) A person or animal.

dairy (DER-ee) Having to do with animals that are raised for their milk.

explorer (ek-SPLOR-er) A person who travels and looks for new land.

maple syrup (MAY-pel SUR-up) A sweet food made from the sap of maple trees.

millions (MIL-yunz) Thousands of thousands.

original (uh-RIJ-uh-nul) There from the start.

populated (PO-pyuh-layt-ed) Lived in.

products (PRAH-dukts) Things that are made.

protect (pruh-TEKT) To keep safe.

republic (rih-PUH-blik) A form of government in which the power belongs to the people.

scuba divers (SKOO-buh DY-verz) People who dive with tools that help them breathe underwater.

tourism (TUR-ih-zem) A business that deals with people who travel for pleasure.

Vermont State Symbols

State Tree
Sugar Maple

State Animal
Morgan Horse

State Flag

State Bird
Hermit Thrush

State Flower
Red Clover

State Seal

Famous People from Vermont

John Deere
(1804–1886)
Born in Rutland, VT
Inventor and
Businessman

Calvin Coolidge
(1872–1933)
Born in Plymouth
Notch, VT
U.S. President

Hannah Teter
(1987–)
Born in Belmont, VT
Snowboarder

Vermont State Map

Lake Memphremagog

Lake Champlain

Lamoille River

● Burlington

Winooski River

★ Montpelier

Green Mountains

Connecticut River

Otter Creek

Legend

○ Major City

★ Capital

〜 River

Vermont State Facts

Population: About 608,827

Area: 9,609 square miles (24,887 sq km)

Motto: "Freedom and Unity"

Song: "These Green Mountains," words and music by Diane Martin

Index

Web Sites

Due to the changing nature of Internet links, PowerKids Press has developed an online list of Web sites related to the subject of this book. This site is updated regularly. Please use this link to access the list:
www.powerkidslinks.com/amst/vt/